JESUS IN THE QURAN

Also by Qazi Fazl Ullah

Sharia & Politics

Science of Hadith

Hajj & Umrah According to All Four Schools of Jurisprudence

Jihad: Why, How, & When

Sayyidah Aaisha: Age & Marriage

Ramadan: Components of the Holy Month

JESUS IN THE QURAN
WRITTEN BY **QAZI FAZL ULLAH**
EDITED BY **EVELYN THOMPSON**

HUND INTERNATIONAL PUBLISHING
LOS ANGELES, CALIFORNIA
2018

COPYRIGHT © 2018 BY QAZI FAZL ULLAH

All rights reserved. This book or any portion thereof may not be reproduced or used in any manner whatsoever without the express written permission of the publisher except for the use of brief quotations in a book review or scholarly journal.

FIRST PRINTING: 2018

ISBN: 978-1-732-60173-4

HUND INTERNATIONAL PUBLISHING

LOS ANGELES, CALIFORNIA

PRINTED IN THE UNITED STATES OF AMERICA

TABLE OF CONTENTS

PREFACE 9

HUMANS : A UNIQUE CREATURE 11

ALLAH, MESSAGE, AND THE MESSENGER 14

DEEN AND MESSAGE 17

JESUS *[ISA]* IN THE *HOLY QURAN* 22

MARYAM [MARY], THE MOTHER OF JESUS *[ISA]* 25

MARYAM AND *ZAKARIYYAH* [MARY AND ZACHARIAH] 27

ZAKARIYYAH AND *YAHYA* [ZACHARIAH AND JOHN] 28

MARYAM [MARY] IS A CHOSEN WOMAN 30

MARYAM [MARY] AND BIRTH OF JESUS *(ISA)* 32

JESUS *(ISA)* LIFTED ALIVE 34

MARYAM [MARY] AND BIRTH OF JESUS *(ISA)* 36

ZAKARIYYAH (ZACHARIAH) AND *YAHYA* [JOHN] 41

BIRTH OF *YAHYA* [JOHN] ITS SUPPORTIVE EVIDENCE 44

MARYAM'S CHASTITY 50

ISA [JESUS] IS A MESSENGER OF *ALLAH* 51

JESUS [*ISA*] AND CHRISTIANITY 60

ALLAH HAS NO CHILDREN 69

CONCEPT OF CRUCIFICTION 72

THE SIGNS OF THE HOUR 78

THE RETURN OF JESUS [*ISA*] 84

JESUS'S (*ISA'S*) MIRACLES 88

DAY OF JUDGEMENT AND JESUS [*ISA*] 90

BOOKS BY *QAZI FAZL ULLAH* 97

ABOUT THE AUTHOR 111

PREFACE

Allah the almighty created the entire world, created humans as the honored creature, and subjugated to them the world and the things therein to exploit it for their benefit. On the other hand, he made them bound to follow his commandments in each and every aspect of their life. By doing so, we will live in peace, harmony, and tranquility in this world and enjoy a prosperous life in the hereafter.

For the said purpose he sent 124,000 *Prophets* and *Messengers* to us. They received *Wahi* [revelation] from *Allah* and conveyed it to the people. They not only taught, but acted as role models as well. People are bound to follow them, their words, and their actions in words and spirit with full sincerity.

From Adam to Jesus *(Isa),* the Prophets were sent in different areas to different peoples and nations. Their basic message was the same: belief in the oneness of *Allah,* who has no partner either in his entity nor in his attributes and qualities, nor in his power and actions. He and only he is to be worshipped, and only his power is to be believed in. He is the creator and all others are his creatures. Only he is the lord and all others are his slaves. Only he is to be worshipped and all others must worship him. Then *Allah* sent *Prophet Muhammad* with the same message to the whole world as the end to this process of message and *Messengers* and as its completion and perfection.

Humans and nations were misled due to their ignorance, lack of knowledge and approach, or because of their exceeding love for someone. So, they sometimes believe that a certain creature is God or part of God, or his partner, perhaps because they saw something metaphysical in a creature, so they started worshipping him as if he were God.

In this regard, the case of Jesus *(Isa)* is typical, in that that some of his so-called followers believe that he is God; some others said he is son of God; and some others said he is part of God.

WHO WAS JESUS *(ISA)*?

In this book what the *Holy Quran*, the final message of *Allah*, said about Jesus *(Isa)* is mentioned, and where needed a few *Ahadith* [sayings] of *Prophet Muhammad* have also been quoted as well to make the concept clear.

May *Allah* make it a good effort towards the right faith and right path. *Ameen.*

QAZI FAZL ULLAH

LOS ANGELES, CALIFORNIA

UNITED STATES OF AMERICA

HUMANS : A UNIQUE CREATURE

Allah the almighty has created this whole world and the things therein. He also created human beings as a special creature.

This creature is different than the other animals in bodily structure and features. Most animals walk on four legs. Birds fly, and even the bodies of those that do not, like the chicken two, are structured to be horizontal.

Allah said,

> "Then we created him [humans] as another [unique] creature (23:14)."

Also, *Allah* said,

> "Indeed, we created human in the best of molds [stature] (95:4)."

In a *Hadith* the *Prophet Muhammad* said,

> "Allah created Adam in his shape."

"His shape" either means Adam's shape, meaning a new and unique shape, or it means in *Allah's* image. But *Allah* does not have any form or shape, so it means that *Allah* used a specially selected shape for creating Adam, and for sure that is and will be the best shape.

Basically, humans are a type of animal who shares all the same qualities, needs, and habits as animals, like eating and drinking. Human brains are built in three sections, which are described below:

a. Brain system which is the lowest chamber (amygdala), it gives natural motion to the vital organs like the hearts, kidneys, liver, lung, etc. that are required to maintain life.

b. Limbic system – Emotions and feeling comes like fear, love, anger, mercy, etc. are generated here. These two systems also have in their brain.

c. Cerebral cortex. This chamber is developed in humans only and not in other animals, and here is found the intellect.

This intellect is human's distinction. Through this intellect he is honored to exploit the world and the things therein, from the soil to the sun.

Allah said,

> *"And indeed, we have honored the children of Adam and we have given them control over land and ocean and provided them pure things and given them virtue [priority] over a lot of what we created, with a great priority [17:70]."*

Also, *Allah* said,

"Allah is the one who has created the heavens and the earth and sent down water from the sky, so he brought forth there with fruits [grains, etc.] as sustenance for you and he made the ships subject to you, in order to sail in the sea by his leave and made the rivers subject to you, and he subjugated for you the sun and the moon diligently pursuing their course and subjugated for you the night and day and provided for you whatever you need and if you count the favors of Allah you cannot number it indeed human is unjust and ungrateful [14:32-34]."

ALLAH, MESSAGE, AND THE *MESSENGER*

BELIEF IN THE LORDSHIP OF *ALLAH*, MESSAGE, AND *MESSENGERS*

Verses like those above express that when humans are given the status and talent to exploit all these things then they are bound to believe in the lordship of *Allah* and to obey his commandments, as *Allah* has put this in their nature.

Allah said,

> *"And [remember] when your lord drew forth from the children of Adam from their loins, their descendants and made them witness to themselves, [asking them] am I not your lord? They said yes, we testify [Admit]. Lest you should say on the day of resurrection 'of this we were not aware of (7:172).'"*

Now this thing is there in the intuition and sub-consciousness of everyone, as this promise was inscribed into our souls.

Then all the *Messengers* and *Prophets* are sent to humans to remind them of their covenant.

In that world of souls, *Allah* also extracted a promise from his *Messengers* for another issue, as he said,

> "Behold! Allah took a covenant of the Prophets saying, for sure I will give you a book and wisdom and then came to you a Messenger confirming what is with you [the basic message and its contents] for sure you may believe in him and help him. He said did you admit and take my covenant as a binding one. They say we admit. He said then bear witness and I am with you among the witnesses (3:81)."

Then every *Messenger* and *Prophet* told his followers about this coming *Messenger* and everyone received their covenant as well.

Allah is merciful, and the message and *Messenger* is his mercy, as he said,

> "And they said, 'Why is not this Quran sent down to a great man of these two cities [Makkah and Ta'if]?' (43:31)."

Then *Allah* said,

> "Is it they who will portion out the mercy of your lord (43:32)."

It means that the message is the mercy of *Allah*, and *Allah* wills people to follow his guidance to avoid punishment. So, he did not leave any room for any excuse in this regard, as he said,

> "[He sent] Messengers as bringers of good news as well as warners. So, mankind may not have any plea [excuse]

against Allah after [his sending of the Messengers] 4:165)."

DEEN AND MESSAGE

Allah has sent only one *Deen* (religion) and that is *Islam*.

> "Indeed, Deen to Allah is Islam (3:19)."

> "And whoever seeks besides Islam any Deen it will never be accepted of him and he in the hereafter will be of the losers (3:85)."

Islam means submission to the will of *Allah*, and all the *Messengers* called people towards that.

Allah said,

> "He enjoined on you of Deen He [Allah] enjoined on Nuh [Noah] and that which we had enjoined on Ibrahim [Abraham], Musa [Moses], and Isa [Jesus] to implement it and make no division in it [i.e., make no sects therein or make no pick and choose therein, as this is a package deal] (42:13)."

So *Deen* is one and the same. However, laws and rules differ in different times according to situation and circumstances, as He said,

> "To each of you we have prescribed a Shariah [law] and clear way (5:48)."

Also, *Allah* said,

> "For every nation we have ordained religious ceremonies, which they follow so they may not dispute with you on this matter, and invite you towards your lord. Verily you are on the straight guidance (17:67)."

So, this *Deen* is the *Deen* of all the *Prophets* and *Messengers*, which was processed towards perfection and completion through all these *Messengers* and their message, until it was completed with the message of *Prophet Muhammad*, the last and final *Prophet* of *Allah*,

as *Allah* said,

> "This day I have perfected for you your Deen and completed on you my favor and chosen for you Islam as "Deen" (system) (5:3)."

So, all these *Prophets* and *Messengers* belong to the same group.

Allah said,

> "And this group [of Messengers] is your group and I am your lord so worship me [alone] (21:92)."

This he mentioned after that he related the stories of a few of them and right after that he said,

> *"But they [the people] cut off their Deen amongst them [i.e., into sects and pieces]; all of them will return to us (21:93)."*

Also, he said after related some stories of them,

> *"And indeed, this group [of the Messengers] is our group, the one group and I am your lord so fear me (23:52)."*

And again, right after he said,

> *"So, they [the people] cut off their Deen amongst them to pieces [sects]. Every group rejoices what is with them (23:53)."*

All these *Messengers* and *Prophets* were sent to a specific tribe or nation, which is seen clearly when they said

> *"O my nation! O my nation!"*

This was said by *Nuh* [Noah], *Hud*, *Saleh*, and *Shoaib*.

> *"We had certainly sent Noah to his people, and he said, "O my people, worship Allah; you have no deity other than Him. Indeed, I fear for you the punishment of a tremendous Day (7:59)."*

> *"And to the 'Aad [We sent] their brother Hud. He said, "O my people, worship Allah; you have no deity other than Him. Then will you not fear Him? (7:65)"*

> *"And to the Thamud [We sent] their brother Salih. He said, "O my people, worship Allah; you have no deity*

other than Him. There has come to you clear evidence from your Lord. This is the she-camel of Allah [sent] to you as a sign. So, leave her to eat within Allah's land and do not touch her with harm, lest there seize you a painful punishment (7:73)."

"And to [the people of] Madyan [We sent] their brother Shuaib. He said, "O my people, worship Allah; you have no deity other than Him. There has come to you clear evidence from your Lord. So, fulfill the measure and weight and do not deprive people of their due and cause not corruption upon the earth after its reformation. That is better for you, if you should be believers (7:85)."

But the last and final *Prophet* of *Allah*, *Prophet Muhammad*, always addressed humans in general and said

"Say (O Muhammad!) O Mankind I am the Messenger of Allah to all of you...(7:158)"

and that applies from his time until the last day of this world.

So, this *Deen* is,

1) the *Deen* of Allah,

2) the *Deen* of all the *Messengers* 3,

3) and the *Deen* of humanity in general,

as *Prophet Muhammad* has been sent as the last and final *Messenger* to the whole world and to all humans in all times until the end of the world.

And as we said that the base of this *Deen* is *Tauheed*, or belief in the oneness of *Allah*, as *Allah* said,

> *"And we have not sent any Messenger But we used to reveal to him that there is no God [to be worshipped] but only me, so worship me [alone] (21:25)."*

And every one of them performed his duty in the proper way. They never compromised on this basic issue of their message, even though they suffered for it, they were tortured and even some of them were killed.

A compromise takes place, either out of fear or because of vested interest, but these *Messengers* never had any fear; nor did they have any other interest, but only to perform their duties accordingly to fulfill their obligations and to please their Lord.

JESUS [*ISA*] IN THE *HOLY QURAN*

In the *Holy Quran* the names of only 25 *Messengers* are mentioned and Jesus *(Isa)* is one of them. His name in Arabic is *Isa,* but sometimes his title *"Maseeh" [Messiah]* is mentioned. Also, he is mentioned as *Ibni Maryam* [son of Mary], and this is to reject the wrong concepts about him, such as the notion that he is the son of God as the Christians say, or the illegitimate son of *Yusuf Najjar* [Joseph the Carpenter], as is the Jewish point of view.

HOW WAS JESUS *(ISA)* BORN?

Allah, the sole creator of the world, created it and he has created and established for its smooth running the physical rules and procedure. Every atom, particle and thing is functioning accordingly to what it has been created for. This has been a very stable system from day one.

This is called *Tadbeer*, which literally means *"planning."* It means things are functioning in accordance to the planning of its creator. That is why one attribute or quality name of *Allah* is *Mudabbir* (one who plans).

Allah said that,

> "If you O Prophet, ask them [the polytheists] who plans the smooth running of this worldly system? For sure so they will say, Allah (10:31)."

As there is no other answer to this question.

But this is what he planned for this system and he is the creator of this world, the lord of it, and its planner as well, so if he wills sometimes something to happen otherwise, he is able to do anything he wills, and something that happens and that is called miracle, as it happened metaphysically (Means against the physical established system).

Allah said,

> "But Allah does what he intends (2:253)."

> "And Allah does what he wills (14:23)."

So, *Allah* can give life to dead as he causes death, but human beings by nature inclined to trust their senses and intellect, so most of them believe in these findings more than they believe in what the creator says. It is because of their ignorance of that sense and intellect have its own limits and they sense and know very little, while a lot is beyond its approach even in physical world and physics.

Allah said,

> "And you have not been given of knowledge but very little (17:82)."

Qudrat [power] is the eternal attribute of *Allah* and it means its perfection and completion, so nothing is beyond or out of his *Qudrat*.

MARYAM [MARY], THE MOTHER OF JESUS [*ISA*]

Maryam is from the offspring of *Ibrahim* [Abraham] through *Ishaq* [Isaac] and *Yaqub* [Jacob]. Her father is *Imran*, son of *Hashim*, son of *Amun*.

Allah says,

> "*Verily Allah has chosen Adam, Nuh [Noah], the family of Ibrahim and the family of Imran above the Aalameen [creatures] offspring, of one another. And Allah is all-hearing, all-knowing (3:33-34).*"

The mother of *Maryam*, *Hannah*, daughter of *Faqub*, could not have children. One day she saw a bird feeding its chicks, and she wished for a child and prayed to *Allah*.

Allah says,

> "*[Remember] when the wife of Imran said, 'O my Lord! I have vowed to you what is in my womb to be dedicated*

for your services, so accept this from me. Verily you are all-hearing, all-knowing.' Then when she gave birth, she said, 'O my Lord! I have given birth to a female child and Allah knew better what she delivered. And the male is not like the female, and I have named her, Maryam [Mary] and I seek refuge with you for her and for her offspring from Satan the outcast (3:35-36)."

Let us consider the words

"and Allah knew what she delivered."

This *"what"* means refers to the great character of the child she delivered. Also, the wording,

"and the male is not like the female"

means no male person is like this woman. This is a great woman. These two things *Allah* said regarding *Maryam*.

MARYAM AND *ZAKARIYYAH* [MARY AND ZACHARIAH]

"So, her Lord [Allah] accepted her with a goodly acceptance. He made her grow in a good manner and put her under the care of Zakariyyah [Zachariah]. Every time Zakariyyah entered the mihrab [secluded room] to visit her, he found her supplied with sustenance. He said, 'O Maryam, from where have you gotten this?' She said, 'This is from [Allah].' Verily Allah provides sustenance to whom he wills without limits (3:37).'"

ZAKARIYYAH AND YAHYA [ZACHARIAH AND JOHN]

After this, *Allah* mentions the story of *Zakariyyah*.

Allah said,

> "Here [at that time and in that place] Zakariyyah invoked his lord, saying, 'O my Lord! Grant me from you a good offspring, as you are indeed the all hearer of invocation.' So, the angels called him while he was standing praying in the Mehrab [separate vaulted room], that Allah gives you the glad tidings of Yahya [John], confirming the word from Allah, a Sayyid [noble], Hasoor [confined to worship meaning a devout worshipper]. And a Prophet from amongst the righteous. He said, "O my Lord! How will I have a son when I am very old and my wife is barren?" Allah replied, "Thus Allah does what he wills." Zakariyyah said, "O my Lord! Give me a sign." Allah said, "Your sign is that you will not speak to people for three days, but [communicate] with signs. And remember your

> *Lord a lot and glorify [him] in the afternoon and in the morning (3:39-41)."*

Zakariyyah and his wife both were quite old. Normally at their age, there is no possibility of pregnancy, but when *Zakariyyah* saw that *Maryam* was getting provisions without any physical mean or source, he found that *Allah* not only can do everything, but he does when he wills, literally and metaphysically. So, he asked for a son and as in normal procedure the signs of pregnancy seen on a woman, but this was a metaphysical and abnormal happening, so *Allah* told him that the sign would be on him and that he would not be able to speak for three days and nights. Also, the words

> *"confirming the word from Allah"*

means that when a son would be born to *Zakariyyah's* wife at such an advanced age, this would be sufficient as confirmation for the birth of Jesus *(Isa)* without a father, as both would be impossible physically. It is also a preparation for the birth of Jesus *(Isa)*, as the people never made an objection to the birth of *Yahya* [John] in similar circumstances, so why should there be an objection to the birth of Jesus *(Isa)*?

MARYAM [MARY] IS A CHOSEN WOMAN

After this story, *Allah* said,

> "And [remember] when the angels said, 'O Maryam! Verily Allah has chosen you, purified you and chosen you over the women of the nations. O Maryam! Submit yourself with obedience to your Lord and prostrate yourself and bow down along with those who bow down (3:42-43).'"

These verses made it clear that *Maryam* was of the chosen women.

Now when *Prophet Muhammad* gave all these news in detail while he was not a literate man and had never studied nor learnt nor read anything about these details, then that is sufficient proof that he was a *Messenger* of *Allah*,

as He said,

> "This is from the news of the Ghaib [things one cannot find either through the use of senses or by one's powers of intellect], which we reveal to you. You were not with

> them, when they were casting lots with their pens as to which of them should be charged with the care of Maryam, nor were you with them when they were disputing [who should charge of her care] (3:44)."

It is said that their dispute was due to their respect for their *Imam* [religious leader, who in this case was *Imran*, the father of *Maryam*]; everyone wanted to take care of the daughter of their *Imam* and *Zakariyyah* said,

> "I am prior to everyone as her maternal aunt is my wife, and an aunt is second to the mother [In Islamic Shariah, aunts are second only to mothers in terms of deference]."

But others did not heed this argument. So, they agreed on a draw for the dispute to be settled. So, they threw their pens made of reed in *River Jordan* to see whose pens will not go with the flow of the water, but in the opposite direction, and some scholars said that whoever's pens will remain vertical in the water, he will take care of her, so in that way *Zakariyyah* was awarded her care.

MARYAM [MARY] AND BIRTH OF JESUS *(ISA)*

After this *Allah* said to *Maryam* through inspiration,

"And [remember] when the angels said o Maryam [Mary] verily Allah gives you the glad tidings of word from him, his name will be Al-Masih [Messiah] Isa [Jesus] the son of Maryam [Mary] held in honor in this world and in the hereafter, and he will be one of those who are near to all. He will speak to the people from the cradle and as a Kahl and he will be one of the righteous." She said, "O my Lord! How will I have a son when no man has touched me?" He said, "The same way Allah creates what he wills: when he decrees something. He says to it only, 'Be!' And it is, and he will teach him the book [in writing], the wisdom, the Taurat [Torah] and the Injeel [Gospel]. And (saying that) as a Messenger to the children of Israel I have come to you with a sign from your Lord. I will fashion for you out of clay a figure of a bird and breathe into it and it will become a bird by Allah's leave, and I heal the blind and the leper and I bring the dead to life by Allah's leave. And I inform you of what

you eat and what you store in your houses. Surely, therein in is a sign for you if you believe. [And I have come] confirming that which was before me in the Taurat and make lawful to you a part of what was forbidden to you, and I have come to you with a proof from your Lord. So have fear of Allah and follow me. Indeed, Allah is my Lord and our Lord so worship him, this is the straight path (3:45-51)."

JESUS (*ISA*) LIFTED ALIVE

AND THUS, WAS JESUS *(ISA)* LIFTED ALIVE.

In these verses it is mentioned that *Allah* inspired *Maryam* [Mary] about her son and what he would be doing. Here also it is mentioned that he will speak to people in the cradle, but cradle is mentioned as a metaphor as infants are mostly in cradle otherwise it means in his infancy. Now the word *Kahlan* means and in *Kahoolat* as well. And that is the age of forty and plus. Now all humans almost speak in a *Kahoolat*, but when *Allah* specifically mentioned Jesus *(Isa)* speaking in *Kahoolat* in the same context of speaking in his cradle, which means this speaking of Jesus *(Isa)* in *Kahoolat* is unique thing.

Now when Jesus *(Isa)* was lifted to the heavens when his enemies tried to crucify him, he was a young man of thirty-three years, and that is not the age of *Kahoolat*. It comes later in life, which implies that Jesus *(Isa)* will speak to people in this world later when he will be *Kahl*. It means that he is alive and he will come back. We will discuss this later.

Allah also related to *Maryam* that her son Jesus [*Isa*] will perform miracles and these are:

- Making a figure of a bird from clay, breathing in it, and turning it into a flying bird;

- healing the lepers and blind with no medicine;

- bringing the dead to life;

- informing his people of what they eat and what they store with no prior knowledge of it.

Now apparently all these are the actions of *Allah* and only his power. And that is why he said when he performed all these actions,

"With the leave of Allah,"

which means

"This is not in my hands, it is not my power, Allah will be doing this through me, and all this is metaphysical."

Also, he will be making it clear that he will be a *Messenger* confirming *Taurat* [Torah] and the miracles and *Injeel* as proof of being a *Messenger* and he will finish his speech that *Allah* is his Lord and yours as well, which means he submits to *Allah* as his Lord and admits that he is his slave.

MARYAM [MARY] AND BIRTH OF JESUS *(ISA)*

Regarding *Maryam* and her giving birth to Jesus *(Isa)*,

Allah said,

> *"And mention in the book Maryam [Mary], when she withdrew in seclusion from her family to a place facing east. She put a curtain [screen] between her and them, then we sent to her our Ruh [spirit], meaning the angel Jibril [Gabriel], and he appeared before her in the form of a man in all respects. She said, "Verily I seek refuge with the most gracious from you, if you do fear Allah." He [the angel] said, "I am only a Messenger from your Lord to announce to you the gift of a righteous son." She said, "How will I have a son when no man touched me, nor am I unchaste?" He said, "Like this your lord said that is for me and to appoint him as a sign to mankind and a mercy from us and this matter has been decreed. So, she conceived Isa and she withdrew with him to a far place. Then the pain of childbirth drove her to the trunk of a date palm. She said, "Would that I had died before this and had been forgotten and out of sight! (19:16-39)"*

Then he [Angel *Jibril* or the newborn baby Jesus] cried out from under her,

> "Grieve not. Your lord has provided a stream of water under you. And shake the trunk of date palm towards you; it will let fresh ripe dates fall upon you. So eat, drink and cool down your eye [meaning be happy with by your baby], and if you see any human being, say, 'Verily I have vowed fast unto the beneficent [Allah], so I shall not speak to any human being this day.'"

When Jesus [*Isa*] was born she carried him to her people.

They said,

> "O Mary! Indeed, you have brought a very mighty [false] thing. O sister of Harun [Aaron], your father was not a man who used to commit adultery, nor was your mother an unchaste woman."

So, she pointed to him.

They said,

> "How can we speak to a child in a cradle?"

Jesus *(Isa)* said,

> "Verily I am a slave of Allah. He has given me the Scripture and made me a Prophet, and he has made me blessed. Whosoever I be, and has enjoined on me the prayer and Zakat [charity] as long as I live, dutiful to my mother and made not arrogant or unjust. And peace be

upon me, the day I was born the day I die, and the day I shall be raised alive. It is not for Allah to beget a child. Glory be to him whenever he decreed an issue, he says to it be and that is. And verily Allah is my Lord and your Lord, this is the straight path. Then the sects different amongst them so woe unto the disbelievers from the meeting of the great day. What a good hearer they will be, and a good seer. And warn them of the day of grief and regrets when the case would be decided while they are in a state of carelessness and they do not believe (19:30-39)."

THESE VERSES MAKE IT CLEAR THAT JESUS *(ISA)* WAS BORN WITHOUT A FATHER, BUT HOW?

We mentioned before that *Allah* created the whole world, and he created and established the natural system. The world is running in accordance to that system.

Allah says,

> *"And verily we have created above you seven heavens and we are not careless of the creature (23:17)."*

It means that he guards the whole world. And he is the creator, and lord of the whole world, so when he wills something otherwise it happens that way, means not in accordance to its physical process.

Allah said,

> *"And he does what he wills (14:27)."*

Now it is a natural and physical procedure that male and female meet and then she conceive a baby. But all this comes due to the rules he has established in his creature, and when he wills he can create without this process. Self-pollination takes place in several plants and trees. Certain worms, bees and birds give birth to their larvae and lay eggs through parthenogenesis, meaning without meeting of male and female. It can be that in the case of Jesus (*Isa*) this process took place. This is only to answer the objection. Then for things to be possible physically, these natural rules are related to the creature and not for the creator. In the kingdom the king is not subject to the laws made in his name, then how can the creator be subject to the rules of the created. So, *Isa* was born without a father, as the creator created him in this way.

Then something was in the mind of *Maryam*, when she said,

"How will I give birth to a baby without been touched by a male?"

and the angel told her,

"Your lord said this is easy for me,"

meaning that as all other things there is no difficulty for *Allah* at all to do this. And as this happened metaphysically, which is why her people also brought forth their reservations and even objections to confirm this metaphysical thing. *Allah* empowered the newborn baby *Isa* to speak of himself eloquently and he also mentioned in his statement that he is to be sent as a *Prophet* and would be given Scripture as well. And as his birth and his speech when he was a newborn baby was beyond the approach of people, he made it clear that no one should believe in him as lord, so he said that *Allah* is his lord and our lord as well.

Now they saw him speak in such a time and for sure that was from *Allah*, his birth without a father was also from *Allah* in the same way.

ZAKARIYYAH (ZACHARIAH) AND YAHYA [JOHN]

Here in this *Surah* [chapter] *Allah* also related the story of *Zakariyyah* and *Yahya*.

Allah says (19:1-15),

> "*Kaf Ha Ya Ain Sad* [this is] mentioning [story] of the mercy of your lord to his slave Zakariyyah when he called out to his lord in loneliness."

He said,

> "My lord, indeed my bones have grown feeble and gray hair has spread on my head and I have never been unblessed in my innovation to you, o my lord! And verily I fear my relatives after me and my wife is barren. So, give me from your side an heir who shall inherit me and inherit the offspring of Yaqub [Jacob] and make him o my lord! A beloved one."

Allah said,

> "O Zakariyyah, we give you the glad tidings of a son whose name is Yahya [John]. We have not given this name to anyone before him."

Zakariyyah said,

> "My Lord! How will I have a son when my wife is barren and I have reached such extreme old age?"

Allah said,

> "So, your lord said, that is easy for me. Certainly, I created you when you were nothing."

Zakariyyah said,

> "O my lord! Give me a sign."

Allah said,

> "Your sign is that you will not be able to speak unto mankind for three nights."

So, he came out to his people from *Al Mihrab* [the seclusion and worship room] then he told them [with signs] to glorify *Allah* in the morning and in the afternoon. Then *Yahya* (John) was born and *Allah* ordered him,

> "O Yahya! Hold the Scripture [Torah] fast. I will give you wisdom and power to decide or to judge while you are a child, pure and a pious and dutiful towards your parents,"

and he was neither arrogant nor disobedient and *Salam* [peace] be on him, the day he was born, the day he dies, and the day he will be raised up to life.

BIRTH OF *YAHYA* [JOHN] ITS SUPPORTIVE EVIDENCE

This birth of *Yahya* for *Zakariyyah* and his wife in such an old age and the sterility of his wife was a precedent for the birth of *Isa* (Jesus) without father, as both cases prove the power of *Allah*, that he can do anything, but as the birth of *Isa* (Jesus) was beyond their approach regarding the power of *Allah*, which is why the people adopted different views regarding *Isa* (Jesus).

PEOPLE DIFFERED

Allah said,

> *"Then the sects differed so woe unto the disbelievers from their attendance of the great day (19:37)."*

Where they will come to know the facts, and will admit that they were wrong as *Allah* said,

> *"How good a hearer they will be and how good a seer [on that day] but these wrongdoers today are in a plain error. "And warn them [O Muhammad] of the day of grief when the issue would be decided." But they are in carelessness and they do not believe (19:38-39)."*

And to make the issue completely understandable,

Allah said,

> *"Verily the likeness of Isa before Allah is the likeness of Adam. He created him from dust then he said to him be! And he was. [This is] the truth from your lord, so be not of those who doubt (3:59-60)."*

The creation of Adam from dust was much stranger than the birth of *Isa* (Jesus) without a father. Then this denial and refusal of them more arrogance.

Allah said,

> *"Then whoever disputes with you concerning him after this knowledge has come to you, then say let us call our sons and your sons over women, and your women, ourselves and yourselves then we put the curse of Allah upon who lie verily this is the true narratives and there is no "Ilah" [god to be worshipped or to be called as "Rab" [Lord] but only Allah, and verily Allah is the al-mighty, the all-wise, then if they will turn away then Allah is all aware of those who do mischief (3:61-63)."*

Allah said,

> *"And we made the son of Maryam and his mother as a sign and we gave them refuge on high ground, a place of rest, security and flowing stream. O Messengers! Eat of lawful pure things and practice righteous deeds, verily I am well acquainted with what you do and verily this your religion is one religion and I am your lord, so keep your duty to me (23:50-53)."*

Then they [the people] broke their religion amongst them unto sects, each group rejoicing with what they had.

Allah said,

> *"And remember Zakariyyah when he invoked his Lord, 'O my lord leave me not single [without children] for you are the best of the inheritors.' So we answered his call and we cured his wife and we bestowed upon him Yahya. Verily they used to hasten on to do good deeds and they used to call on us with hope and fear, and used to humble themselves before us and the woman [Mary] who guarded her chastity we breathed into her [sleeves] our Ruh [spirit] and we made her and her son Jesus a sign for people. Truly this ummah is your ummah [group/faith/laws] and I am your lord therefore worship me alone (21:89-93)."*

Then they broke up their religion amongst them.

These verses said that people later made certain concepts and took them as their *Deen* [religion] while *Deen* and the faith therein is one and only one, and the people also argued and divided over what *Allah* said regarding *Isa's* (Jesus's) birth without a father, his speech as a new born baby, and his miracles. The Jews said that he was an illegitimate son of *Yusuf An Najjar* [Joseph the carpenter], while those who claimed to follow *Isa* (Jesus) believed that he is God or he is a part of God, or he is son of god, while he is a human and a *Messenger* of *Allah*, having been born without a father, speaking when he was a newborn baby, performing miracles, announcing his slavery to *Allah* and believing in *Allah*. So, *Allah* said regarding those who say otherwise,

> *"So, leave them [O Muhammad] in their error for a time. Do they think that in wealth and children with which we enlarge them we hasten unto them with good things? Nay, but they do not conceive [that this is a test and trial for them] (23:54-56)."*

Also, *Allah* said regarding those who believe in the proper way will be rewarded.

> *"So whosoever does righteous good deeds and he is a believer his efforts will not be rejected and verily we record it for him (21:94)."*

So what people believed regarding *Isa*, Prophet Muhammad made this position clear, and *Allah* has ordered to believe in what he said,

> *"O mankind verily there has come to you the Messenger [Muhammad] with truth from your lord, so believe in him it is better for you, but if you disbelieve then certainly to Allah belongs all that is in the heavens and on earth, and Allah is all knowing, all wise (4:170)."*

Then *Allah* ordered people of the book not to cross over the boundaries regarding *Deen* and beliefs.

> "O people of the scripture, do not exceed the limits in your religion, nor say of Allah aught but the truth. The Messiah Isa son of Mary was a Messenger of Allah as was his word, which he bestowed on Maryam and a Ruh [spirit] from him. So believe in Allah and his Messengers. Say not (gods are) three [The Trinity], cease! [It is] better for you. Allah is the only one God. Glory be to him; [he is above] having a son. To him belongs all that is in the heavens and all that is on earth, and Allah is all sufficient as a disposer of the affairs (4:17)."

After this *Allah* says that,

> "The Messiah will never be proud, to reject to be a slave of Allah nor the angels who are near [to Allah]. And whosoever rejects his worship in pride and thinks of himself very high, then he will gather them all together unto himself. So as for those who believed and practiced good deeds, he will give them their rewards and more of his bounty. And those who refused and showed pride, he will punish them with painful torment and they will not find for themselves against Allah any protection nor helper. O mankind! Verily there has come to you a convincing proof from your lord and he sent down to you a manifest light. So those who believed in all and held fast to him he will admit them to his mercy and grace and guide them to himself straight path (4:172-175)."

In these verses *Allah* said that Jesus (*Isa*) is the *Messenger* of *Allah*. He was born in a metaphysical way with by the word of *Allah* and Jesus himself does not reject being the slave of *Allah*, so calling him the son of God is wrong, as *Allah* has neither part nor partner; he attends to all affairs on his own.

MARYAM'S CHASTITY

Regarding *Maryam* and her chastity,

Allah says,

> "and Maryam, daughter of Imran, who guarded her chastity, so we breathed in her [sleeves] our Ruh [spirit] and she confirmed the words of her lord [that she got pregnant with this word] and the books of Allah [as well, as this was mentioned in the divine books that one of Allah's Messengers would be born without a father] and she was of the obedient people (66:12)."

ISA [JESUS] IS A *MESSENGER* OF *ALLAH*

Isa [Jesus] is a *Messenger* of *Allah* like all other *Messengers*, as *Allah* said,

> "And indeed, we gave Musa [Moses] the book and followed him up with a succession of Messengers. And we gave Isa the son of Maryam clear signs and strengthened him with Ruh Ul Quds [the Holy Spirit Jibril [Gabriel]]. Then whenever there came to you a Messenger with such a thing which yourselves desired not, you became arrogant? Some [of them] you disbelieved and some [of them] you killed (2:87)."

Also, *Allah* mentioned,

> "and we bestowed on him [Abraham], Ishaq [Isaac] and Yaqub [Jacob], everyone we guided and Nuh [Noah] we guided before and from his [Abraham] offspring was Dawud [David], Sulaiman [Solomon], Ayyub [Job], Yusuf [Joseph], Yahya [John], Isa [Jesus, and Ilyas [Elias], each one of them was of the righteous, and Ismail [Ismael], Al Yasa [Elisha], Yunus [Jonah], and Lut [Lot]

> *and every one of them we preferred on Aalameen [creature] and of their forefathers and of their progeny and of their brethren, we chose them and we guided them to the straight path. This is the guidance of Allah, he guides with whom he wills from his slaves, and if they would have joined [others with Allah] then all that they had done would have been ruined. They are people we had given them the book, the system, and the Prophethood, so if these people [of Makkah] are disbelieving this then indeed we have entrusted it to a people who are not disbelievers to it, they are those whom Allah has guided so follow not their guidance. Say, no any compensation I ask for this [message], this is a reminder [admonition] for people (6:84 - 90)."*

Allah said in,

> "These Messengers, we preferred some of them to others to some of them Allah spoke [from behind the screen like Moses] and others he raised to degrees and to Isa [Jesus] the son of Maryam [Mary] we gave clear proof [miracles] and we strengthened him with Ruh Ul Qudus [the Holy Spirit Jibril [Gabriel]] (2:253)."

As for strengthening with *Ruh* [spirit] is concerned, that is for all the believers as well, even though it has degrees of strength, as *Allah* said,

> "You [O Muhammad] will not find any people who believe in Allah and in the last day, befriending them who oppose Allah and his Messenger even though if they are their fathers or their sons or their brothers or their kindred. Such like people Allah has written [inscribed] in

> *their hearts the Iman [faith] and has strengthened them with Ruh [spirit] from himself and he will admit them to gardens, beneath which the rivers flow, dwelling there [forever]. Allah is pleased with them and they are pleased with him, they are the party of Allah. Verily the party of Allah are the successful people (58:33)."*

So, in case of the believers he said the spirit, and in case of Jesus he said the *Holy Spirit*. Now in the *Quran*, the spirit in this regard is Archangel *Jibril* [Gabriel] as *Allah* said,

> *"There in [the night of power] descend the Ruh [spirit, Gabriel] and the angels by Allah's permission (97:4)."*

Also, *Allah* called him the trustworthy *Ruh* [spirit].

Allah said,

> *"And truly this [Quran] is a revelation from the lord of the worlds, which the trustworthy Ruh [spirit i.e. Gabriel] brought down (26:192)."*

But metaphysically this could be said for angels in general, as they do not have physical form. They are spiritual entities and elements made of light. So, in case of the believers, we can say they were strengthened by the angels so they have strength, stability, peace, tranquility, and satisfaction, and they do not feel fear or grief as *Allah* said,

> *"Verily those who said our lord is Allah, then they stood firm, on them the angels descend saying no fear [here] and no grief [in the hereafter] and receive the glad tidings of paradise, you have been promised with (41:30)."*

Then the following verses say,

> *"We are your friends/protectors in the life of this world and in the other one [hereafter] (41:31)."*

So, this verse explained that no fear is regarding this world and no grief about the hereafter. Strengthening with the spirit is for the believers and for Jesus (*Isa*) as well, but as a *Messenger* for him it was on a high level, which means the *Messenger* face any situation with no fear.

Allah said,

> *"And in their [these aforesaid Messengers] footsteps we sent Isa [Jesus] son of Maryam confirming Taurat that had come before him and we gave him the Injeel [Gospel] in it there is guidance and light and confirmation of Taurat, that had come before it, a guidance and admonition for pious people, so let the people of Injeel [Gospel] judge [the matters] by what Allah has revealed therein. And whosoever does not judge by what Allah has revealed, then they are the rebellious people (5:46-57)."*

These verses said that a *Messenger* has been sent after other *Messengers* having the same message, and also it is mentioned here that *Isa* [Jesus] was confirming the original message of *Taurat* [Torah], the scripture given to Moses (*Musa*) the *Messenger* of the Jews, which means that *Isa* [Jesus] was a *Messenger* to *Children Of Israel* to bring them together on the basis of Torah in its original shape after that they perverted it to their wishes and desires, and made sects and became divided and dispersed, as *Isa* [Jesus] said,

> "And [remember] when Isa [Jesus] son of Mary said, "O children of Israel! I am the Messenger of Allah unto you, confirming what was before me [Torah] and giving glad tidings of a Messenger to come after me, whose name is Ahmad [the other name of Prophet Muhammad], but when he came with clear signs they said, 'This is just magic.' And who is more wrong than that one who spoke a lie concerning Allah while he was invited to Islam? And Allah does not guide the wrongdoers. They intend to put off the light of Allah with their mouths, while Allah will perfect his light even though the disbelievers disliked. He is the one who has sent his Messenger with guidance and with the true Deen [religion] to make it prevail over all religions [which are self-fabricated]. Even if the polytheists dislike it (61:6-9)."

Isa (Jesus) is the *Messenger* and *Allah* ordered belief in him so *Allah* made it clear that *Isa* (Jesus) is his *Messenger* like other *Messengers* having brought one and the same message, and that is why he confirmed the *Messengers* before him, their message and their books and especially the Torah, and, he informed his followers and gave them the glad tidings about the last and final *Messenger*, his name is *Ahmad*.

In more than one *Ayat* [verse] *Allah* mentioned *Isa* [Jesus] in the group of his *Messengers*. He ordered his *Messenger Muhammad*,

> "Say [O Muhammad] we believed in Allah and in what has been sent down to us, and what was sent down to Ibrahim [Abraham], Ishmael [Ismail], Ishaq [Isaac], Yaqub [Jacob], and his offspring [the twelve tribes of Israel and their Prophets] and that which was given to

> *Musa [Moses] and Isa [Jesus] and other Prophets from their lord, we made no distinction of anyone of them [faith-wise] and we have submitted to him [Allah] (3:84)."*

So, this is *Islam*, the *Deen* [religion] of all the *Messengers*.

So, *Allah* said after this,

> *"And whosoever seeks a religion other than Islam will never be accepted of him and he is the loser in the hereafter (3:85)."*

In the same way *Allah* ordered us, the followers of *Prophet Muhammad*,

> *"Then if they believed in the like of what you have believed in them they are rightly guided, and if they turn away then they are in [mere] opposition [to you and your religion] so Allah will support you against them, and he is the all-hearer, the all-knower (3:136)."*

Then *Allah* also confirmed that the *Messengers* used to receive the message and same was the case of *Isa* [Jesus].

> *"Verily we have revealed to you as we revealed to Nuh [Noah] and the Prophets after him, and we revealed to Ibrahim, Ismail, Ishaq, Yaqub, the offspring [of Jacob], Isa, Ayyub [Job], Yunus [Jonah], Harun [Aaron], Sulaiman [Solomon] and to Dawud [David], we gave Zabur [psalms], and [we revealed] to the Messengers we have mentioned to you before and the Messengers we*

> have not mentioned to you, and to Musa Allah spoke [from behind the screen], to the Messenger glad tidings and the warning in order that mankind should not have any excuse [plea] against Allah after the Messengers. And Allah is all mighty and all-wise, but Allah testifies to that which he has sent to you [O Muhammad]. He has sent it down with his knowledge [telling all about the post and giving guidance], and the angels testify [the same], and Allah is all sufficient as a witness (4:163-166)."

Then *Allah* said,

> "O people! There has come to you the Messenger [Muhammad] with the truth from your lord, so to believe in him is better for you and if you disbelieve then certainly to Allah belongs all that in the heavens and the earth, and Allah is the all mighty, the all wise (4:170)."

So, this is a call from *Allah* to all human beings in general, and then he specifically addressed their wrong concepts about *Isa* as those who refused him as a *Messenger* said that he is an illegitimate son of *Maryam*, and those who accepted him they believe in him as God or the son of God or part of God,

so *Allah* said,

> "O people of the scripture! Do not exceed the limits in your religion, nor say of Allah aught but the truth. The Messiah Isa son of Mary was a Messenger of Allah and his word [be and he was], which he bestowed on Mary, and a Ruh [spirit] from him. So, believe in Allah and his Messengers. Say not three [trinity], cease! [It is] better

for you. Allah is the only one God. Glory be to him [meaning he is above] than having a son. To him belongs all that in the heavens and all that is on earth, and Allah is all sufficient as a disposer of the affairs (4:171)."

After this *Allah* says that,

"The Messiah will never be proud to reject service to Allah, nor the angels who are near [to Allah] (4:172)."

"And whosoever rejects his worship in pride and thinks of himself very high, then he will gather them all together unto himself. So as for those who believed and practiced good deeds, he will give them their reward and more of his bounty. And those who refused and showed pride, he will punish them with a painful torment and they will not find for themselves against Allah any protector nor helper. O mankind! Verily there has come to you a convincing proof from your lord and he sent down to you a manifest light. So those who believed in all and held fast to him, he will admit them to his mercy and grace and guide them to himself straight path (4:173-4:175)."

And *Allah* commanded people of the book to believe in his last and final *Prophet Muhammad*.

"O you who believed [in your own book and Messenger]! Believe in Allah [in all that he said] and in his Messenger [Muhammad] and in the book he has revealed to his Messenger [Muhammad] and also in the books he revealed

before [him], and whoever disbelieves in Allah, in his angels, in his books, in his Messengers and in the last day, then indeed he has strayed too far (4:136)."

JESUS [ISA] AND CHRISTIANITY

It is known that humans in general have a concept of God in their intuition and subconscious, so most of them do believe in a God in one way or the other. For some of them, when there is no divine guidance, or they have it but they misunderstood it, or mix it with their own desires, then they believe in God in a wrong way or believe in a wrong God. Then when they see something or someone with some extraordinary qualities, they believe it is God, or part of God, or a partner of God. This happened in case of *Isa* (Jesus) in Christianity and of *Uzair* [Ezra] in Judaism.

When the Torah vanished, *Allah* sent *Uzair* (Ezra). *Allah* put the whole Torah in his memory, so he stood up and recited it, and as this was a metaphysical happening, so the Jews said Ezra is the son of God, and by son of God they mean his beloved to such an extent that he has metaphysical powers to do anything which means he is *Rab* [Lord]. *Allah* says,

> *"And the Jews said Ezra is the son of Allah and the Christians said Messiah [Jesus] is the son of God. This is their [mere] saying with their mouths [tongues]. This resembles the saying of those who disbelieved before this [they*

believed in the lordship of certain creatures or they believed angels were the daughters of Allah, meaning that they have metaphysical powers and they can do whatever they want]. Allah has cursed them [those who say such things], how perverse they are (9:30)."

And as the *Ayat* [verse] said, the Christians said the same about Jesus, that he is the son of God. *Uzair* [Ezra] recited the entire Torah from memory and *Isa* (Jesus) was born metaphysically, their religious leaders made for them these concepts.

As *Allah* said,

"They [the Jews and Christians] took their rabbis and their monks to be their lords besides Allah, and they made Messiah Jesus son of Mary as lord, while they were not commanded but to worship only one god. There is no Ilah [God to be worshipped] but only him. He is free [too excellent] than what they attribute to him as partner (9:31)."

Furthermore, He said,

"They want to extinguish Allah's light with their mouths, but Allah will not allow except that his light should be perfected even though the disbelievers disliked it (9:32)."

This is followed by verse,

"He [Allah] is the one who sent his Messenger with guidance and with the true religion to make it prevailing over

all religions [wrong concepts people have adopted as religion and faith] even if the Mushrikeen [polytheist] disliked it (9:33)."

And why did the so-called religious leaders introduced these wrong concepts and showed it as *Deen* [religion] to their people? To make money and have worldly gains.

That is why He said,

"O you who believed! Verily many of the rabbis [of Jews] and monks [of Christians] for sure they eat up the wealth of people falsely and hinder [people] from the right path of Allah, and those who hoard up gold and silver and spend them not in the cause of Allah, give them tidings of a painful torment (9:34)."

And as we mentioned before that *Islam* is the *Deen* of *Allah*, the religion of all the *Messengers* and the religion of and for all humans, which processed through all these *Messengers* and completed with *Prophet Muhammad*,

as *Allah* said,

"He [Allah] has ordained for you the same religion he had ordained for Noah, and the one we revealed to Abraham, Moses, Jesus, to establish this Deen [religion] and make no sects therein (42:13)."

To establish *Deen* means to keep it as it is and not pervert or disfigure it. All this happens when personal interests or prejudice creep in, which cover the eyes and ears, and seal the hearts, and then people become arrogant. They don't want to listen to the truth and facts, so *Allah* said,

> *"So therefore [or towards this one and the same religion] call people to it and stand firm as you have been ordered and follow not their desires and say to them I have believed in what Allah has sent down, [all revealed books] and I have been ordered to do justice amongst you. Allah is our Lord and your Lord, for us are our deeds and for you are your deeds, no arguments between us and you [as you have left the original field and belief so how can there be a debate or discussion] Allah will assemble us all and to him is the final return (42:14)."*

For a debate to find out the truth there must be some common points agreed upon. That will be the common field to have a race there in, otherwise there is no competition, so how there will be someone who won and others who lost.

Allah said,

> *"Say O [the Prophet], O people of this scripture [Jews and the Christians]! Come to the Kalimah [word] that is common between us and you, that we will not worship but only Allah and we will not make anything a partner with him [in any way or any sense] and that none of us shall take others as Ar Rab [lords and gods] besides Allah. Then if they turned away [and did not come to this common ground], then say to them be witness that we are Muslims [who submit to Allah and come to the common ground and believe in every revealed book] (3:62)."*

Ultimately this means that the problem is from your side and not from the *Muslim* side, because *Muslims* do not distinguish between the divine books and the *Messengers*; they believe in all of them. But you the Jews and Christians believe in some and not in others: the Jews believe in Abraham (*Ibrahim*) and Moses (*Musa*) but not in Jesus (*Isa*) and *Muhammad*; and the Christians believe in Abraham, Moses, *Isa*, but not in *Muhammad*; while the *Muslims* believe in all these *Messengers* from *Adam* to *Muhammad*. Because if a *Muslim* will refuse to believe in any one of these *Messengers*, he is not a *Muslim*, even though he believes in Prophet Muhammad.

Allah said,

> *"Verily those who disbelieve in Allah and his Messengers and wish to make a distinction between Allah and his Messengers [believing in Allah and not believing in his Messengers or even in one of them] and say, 'We believe in some and do not believe in some others' and they desire to make a way in between, they are the disbelievers and for sure we have prepared for disbelievers a humiliating torment. And those who believe in Allah and his Messengers and they make no distinction between any of them [faith-wise], we shall give them their rewards. And Allah is ever all-forgiving, most merciful (4:150-152)."*

Christians and their belief regarding Jesus (*Isa*).

As we mentioned before regarding *Prophet* Jesus (*Isa*), some people went to on extreme and some others to another extreme, so those who accepted him adopted in him different concepts and beliefs.

Allah said,

"And from those who said we are Christians we took their covenant but they abandoned a good part of the admonition [message and reminder] we had given to them so we planted amongst them enmity and hatred till the day of resurrection, and Allah will inform them of what they used to do. O people of the book! There has come to you our Messenger [Muhammad] explaining to you much of that which you used to hide from the book and pass over much [not explaining it]. There has come to you from Allah a light [Prophet Muhammad] and a plain book with which Allah guides those who seek his good pleasure, the way of peace; and he brings them out of darkness to the light with his will and guides them to the straight path indeed they disbelieved, who said that Allah is the Messiah, son of Maryam [Mary]. Say [O Muhammad] then who has the least power against Allah if he were to destroy the Messiah son of Maryam [Mary], and his mother and all those who are on earth together? And to Allah belongs the dominion of the heavens and the earth and all that is between them. He creates what he wills and Allah is able to do all things. And the Jews and Christians say, 'we are the children of Allah and his beloved' say, 'why then does he punish you for your sins?' Nay, you are but human beings of those he has created. He forgives whom he will and he punishes whom he will and to Allah belongs the dominion of the heavens and the earth and all that is between them, and to him is the return. O People of the Book [the Jews and Christians] there has come to you our Messenger [Muhammad] explaining to you [the things] after a break of [sending the] Messengers, lest

you say, there came to you no bringer of glad tidings, nor a warner. So now there has come to you a bringer of glad tidings and a warner and Allah is able to do all things (5:14-19)."

"Surely they have disbelieved who say, Allah is the Messiah [Jesus] son of Maryam [Mary], while the Messiah said, O children of Israel! Worship Allah [who is] my Lord and your Lord [as well], whosoever will make a partner for Allah, then for sure Allah has forbidden to him the paradise, and his abode is the fire and for the polytheists there are no helpers. There are those who believed that Allah is the third of three [i.e., believe in the trinity], while there is only one God. And if they did not abstain what they say, then for sure those who disbelieved from amongst them will suffer a painful torment. So will they not repent to Allah and ask forgiveness of him. And Allah is oft-forgiving, most Merciful? (5:72-74)."

Then after this *Allah* said regarding *Isa* [Jesus].

"Messiah [Jesus] son of Maryam [Mary] was no more but a Messenger. Before him passed many Messengers, and his was mother was a woman of truth. They both used to eat food (5:75)."

Note: *"one who eats food"* means that one in need of something from outside to keep body and soul together. So, they are creatures like all other creatures and will die, and anyone like this cannot be a god, a part of a god, his offspring, or his partner. When in the battle of *Uhud*, the *Prophet Muhammad* was injured and fell into a trench and Satan loudly proclaimed his death, the *Muslims* could not hold themselves due to their love for their *Prophet* and started running off the battlefield. Then the *Prophet* received revelation,

> *"And Muhammad is but a Messenger, many Messengers have passed before him, so if he died or be killed, then will you turn [back] on your heels and whosoever will turn back on his heels, he cannot harm Allah even a little, and soon Allah will reward the grateful. And this is not for a person to die but with Allah's leave as a written term [3:144-145]."*

So, he made it clear that the *Messengers* are humans and they will die. One who dies cannot be God, a child of god, or a part of God, but with all his piety or metaphysical things he will be a slave-servant of *Allah*.

That is why *Allah* said after this,

> *"Look how we make the Ayat [issues] clear to them, and then look how they are deluded away."*

As the Christians made them lords so *Allah* said,

> *"Say [O Muhammad] will you worship besides Allah something which has no power either to harm or benefit you? But it is Allah who is All-Hearer, All Knower [5:76]."*

It means that it does not make sense that something does not have the power to harm or benefit, be worshipped and to be believed as God. This is exceeding the limits as he said,

"O people of the book! Exceed not the limits in your Deen [religion], other than the proven [concepts]] and follow not the desires of people who went stray before and who misled many and they strayed from the right path [5:77]."

ALLAH HAS NO CHILDREN

As we mentioned that Christians believe in *Isa* [Jesus] as the son of God, so *Allah* rejected this in many verses.

> *"And the Jews said that Uzair [Ezra] is the son of Allah and the Christians said that the Messiah [Isa] is the son of Allah. That is their saying with their mouths [meaning baseless or nonsensical]. Resembling the saying of those who disbelieved before, curse be on them, how they are deluded from the truth (9:30)."*

> *"They said, 'Allah has begotten a son, glory to Him, he is needless [to any son, partners, or to anything].' To him belongs what is in the heavens and what is on the earth. No evidence [proof] have you for this [concept]. Do you say against Allah what you know not? Say, verily those who invent a lie against Allah will not enjoy success or enjoyment in this world and then to us will be their return, then we shall make them taste the severest torment because they used to disbelieve (10:68-70)."*

"And when they say, 'the Most Gracious [Allah] has begotten a son,' indeed they have brought forth a terrible bad thing, whereby the heavens are to be torn and the earth to be split asunder and the mountains fall in ruins, that they ascribed to the Most Gracious [Allah] a son, while it is not suitable for the Most Gracious [Allah] to beget a son. None in the heavens and the earth but come to the Most Gracious [Allah] as a slave. Verily he knows all of them and has counted them [in sequence] perfectly. And everyone will come to him on the day of resurrection all alone (19:88-95)."

"And they said, the Most Gracious [Allah] has begotten a son. Glory be to him [of progeny] but they [those whom they attribute to Allah as his children] are [His] honored slaves. They cannot go ahead of him in speech, and they act on his command. He knows what is in front of them and what is behind them and they cannot intercede but for those he is pleased with them and they stand in awe for fear of him. And whoever of them will say, 'Verily I am god besides him [Allah,' then that one we shall recompense with hell the same way we recompense the wrongdoer (21: 26-29)."

"Allah has not begotten any son, nor there is any God [as partner with him, otherwise each god would have taken away what he created and some would have overcome the others. Glory be to Allah above all that they attribute to him (23:91-92)."

> "If Allah would have willed to beget a son, he would have chosen whom he willed, of those whom he creates. Glory be to him, He is the only One, The Irresistible (39:4)."

> "And they assigned to him [to Allah] out of his slaves a part [partner/son] verily man is a manifest ingrate [disbeliever] (43:15)."

Allah commanded his *Prophet* (*Muhammad*),

> "Say [O Muhammad!] if the Most Gracious would have a son, then I am the first of worshippers [of Allah, so how would I have denied that, but when I do not believe in it, then it means that Allah does not have any son]. Glory be to the Lord of the heavens and the earth, the Lord of the throne [He is above than all they] ascribe to him (43:81-83)."

Even the *Jinn* (demons), when they believed in *Prophet Muhammad*, said,

> "And that exalted is the majesty of our Lord, has taken neither a wife, nor a son, and that the foolish among us used to say against Allah an enormous falsehood (72:3-4)."

CONCEPT OF CRUCIFICTION

As we said before that *Isa* (Jesus) was from the children of Israel, *Allah* sent him to them to guide them to the right path and to present to them the *Taurat* (Torah), and to correct the perversion they have done in the *Taurat* (Torah) and as they had done that for their vain desires and wishes. So, any *Prophet* who came to them, trying to put them back on the right track, they belied some of them and killed a few of them.

> *"And we gave Isa [Jesus] son of Maryam [Mary] clear signs [that he is the Messenger] and we supported him with Ruh Ul Qudus [Holy Spirit], so whenever there came to you a Messenger with what you yourselves desired not, you became arrogant? Some [of them] you belied and some [others] you used to kill (2:87)."*

So, they plotted the same for *Isa* (Jesus) as well, *Allah* said,

> *"Then when Isa [Jesus] came to know of their disbelief, he said, 'Who will be my helper in the cause of Allah?' The Hawariyyun [disciples] said, 'We are the helpers of Allah, we believe in Allah and bear witness that we are Muslims. Our Lord! We believe in what you have sent*

> *down, and we follow the Messenger [Jesus], so write us down who those who bear witness.' And they plotted [to kill him] and Allah planned [to save him] and Allah is the best planner. When Allah said, O Isa [Jesus] I will take you [intact] and raise you to myself and I will rescue from those who disbelieved and I will make those who followed you [in the right way] above those who disbelieved till the day of resurrection. Then to me is your return and I will judge between you in the matters in which you used to dispute those who disbelieved, then I will punish them with a severe torment in this world and in the hereafter, and they will have no helpers. And those who believed [firmly] and practiced righteous deeds, he will give them their rewards, and Allah does not like the wrongdoers. This is what we recite to you of the verses and the wise reminder (3:52-58)."*

In these verses *Allah* made it clear that *Allah* rescued *Isa* (Jesus) from those who plotted to crucify him and lifted him up to himself intact with body and soul.

Then *Allah* made it much clearer and said,

> *"Because of their breaking the covenant, their rejecting the verses of Allah, their killing of the Prophets unjustly, and of their saying, "our hearts are wrapped [with coverings, meaning we do not understand what you say], but Allah has set a seal upon their hearts because of their disbelief, so they do not believe but very little. And because of their disbelief and of their saying regarding Maryam [Mary] a very big false charge and because of*

their saying [boastfully] that they have killed Messiah Isa [Jesus] son of Maryam [Mary] the Messenger of Allah, while they have neither killed him, nor crucified him, but the matter was confused for them, and verily those who differed there in are in doubt about him [about Jesus, whether they killed him or not] they have no [certain] knowledge of him, they follow but a conjecture only. For sure they killed him not, but Allah raised him [Jesus] to himself and Allah is All Mighty, All Wise. And there are none of the People of the Book but he will believe in him [in Jesus as Allah says regarding him] before his death [means before this man's death, as Allah will show him the reality at the time of his death, or it means before the death of Jesus, which means he never died, but he will come back before the end of this world and the people of the book at that time will believe in him as Allah said it] and on the day of resurrection he will be a witness against them (4:155-159)."

Here in these verses *Allah* has elaborated the issue and made it clear that even though the people plotted to kill Jesus (*Isa*), *Allah* saved him. He will come back and the people will believe in him the proper way.

Allah said,

"And when the son of Maryam [Mary] is mentioned for example, then suddenly your people [Quraysh] cry aloud and say, who is better, our god or he [Jesus]? (43:57-58)."

When *Allah* said,

> "Verily you and what you worship besides Allah are the fuel of hell, you will surely enter it (21:98)."

So, they said, *whether our Gods are better or him [Jesus]* so they were trying to dispute the *Prophet* and create for him a trouble with Christians. That look, he says all Gods will go to hell and *Isa* [Jesus] is one of them, even though *Allah* said,

> "Verily those for whom the good has preceded from us, they are removed there from too far, they will not hear even the slightest sound of it and they will abide therein forever, what they themselves desired. The biggest terror shall not grieve them and the angels will receive them [with greetings] this is that day of yours which you were promised (21:101-103)."

So here when they said,

> "Who is better, our gods or him"

then *Allah* said,

> "They did not mention that but only for a dispute, nay, but they are quarrelsome people [43:58]."

Which means they have nothing to do with Jesus (*Isa*) as they do not believe in him neither as a *Messenger* nor as god and lord, but they mentioned him only for *Fitnah* (to stir up trouble).

Then He said,

> *"He is but a slave [of Allah] we granted our favor to him and we made him an example (role model) for the children of Israel (43:59)."*

Then He said,

> *"And he is [shall be] a known sign for the coming of the hour [means the end of the world, as he will come back before this end]. So have no doubt in it [O the addressee] and follow me [believe in what I said] this is the straight path, and let not Satan hinder you, verily he to you is a plain enemy (43:61)."*

And then *Allah* mentioned how clear a message *Isa* [Jesus] gave, but the people divided themselves into sects regarding him and his message.

> *"And when Isa [Jesus] came with clear signs [and rules], he said, I have come to you with wisdom and to explain to you some of that in which you differ. So fear Allah and obey me; verily Allah is my Lord and your Lord [as well], so worship him. This is the straight path. Then the sects differed amongst themselves, so woe to those who do wrong for they will suffer the torment of a painful day (43:63-65)."*

So, he made it clear to them that he is a servant of *Allah* and his *Messenger* and not a God or Lord, as the Lord is only *Allah*. And *Allah* said that a chosen servant of *Allah* would never ask people to worship him, but they all used to call towards the oneness of *Allah* and his worship.

> "This is not for a human being to whom Allah has given him the book, the system, and the Prophethood, and then he will say to the people, be my worshippers rather than Allah. But be people [slaves/worshippers] of the Lord [Allah] because you used to teach the book and study it [and that book calls towards Allah alone]. And he will not order you to take the angels and the Prophets as Lords. Would he be ordering you disbelief after you submitted to Allah (3:79-80)."

Then *Allah* said regarding *Isa* (Jesus) after that he talked about him that he was a true slave-servant of *Allah*, he has done *Allah* much favor.

> "And verily he [Jesus] is a known sign of the hour [the ending of the world] so have no doubt therein [means in the ending of the world and the signs for that, and of it there is the descending of Jesus from the heaven to the earth]. [He also ordered the Prophets to tell people] and follow me [in Deen and whatsoever I told you in this regard and of it, is that Jesus, the son of Mary, is born of his mother without a father. And that he is a Messenger of Allah, and that the people plotted to assassinate him but Allah lifted him to himself alive. Also, he is there with body and soul and that he will be coming close to the ending of the world and he is one of the major signs of that]. This is the straight path (righteous belief) (43:61)."

THE SIGNS OF THE HOUR

As mentioned that this worldly system has an end, and it is proceeding towards that end. That is why changes are taking place and will continue to do so. Some of these changes are mentioned in *Ahadith*, which are known prophecies, and these are small signs of *Qiyamat*. There are some major signs also mentioned in *Ahadith* as well. When these major signs will appear then acquiring *Iman* or repentance will not be accepted by *Allah*.

Allah said in verses of the *Holy Quran*:

> "Are they waiting to see if the angels come to them, or you Lord [Himself], or certain of the signs of your Lord! The day that certain of the signs of your Lord do come, no good will it do to a soul to believe in them then, if it believed not before nor earned righteousness through its faith. Say: "Wait: we too are waiting (6:158)."

In this subject there are many *Ahadith* of the *Prophet Muhammad*:

HADITH #1:

The hour will not come until you see ten signs:

1) The rising of the sun from the west

2) Smoke

3) Emergence of the beast

4) The emergence of *Gog and Magog*

5) The appearance (return) of *Isa ibn Maryam*

6) The appearance of *Dajjal* (imposter/ Anti-Christ)

7) (8, 9) Three land cave-ins: one in the west, one in the east, and one in the *Arabian Peninsula.*

10) Emergence of fire from the midst of Yemen will drive or gather people, stopping with them whenever they stop for the night or to rest for the day.

[*Muslim, Abu Dawud, Tirmidhi, Nisa'i, Ibn Majah*].

HADITH #2:

The last hour will not commence until the sun rises from the west. When the people witness that, they will all believe. No good will it do a person to believe then, if he believes not before [Fathul Bari].

HADITH #3:

Abdullah Ibn Amr said,

"I have memorized a hadith from the Messenger of Allah, which I never forgot afterward, that the first of the signs to appear would be the rising of the sun from the west and the emerging of the beast to mankind in the forenoon. Whichever of them appear first, the other will follow close behind it (Ahmad, Muslim)."

HADITH #4:

Three if they appear, then a soul will not benefit from its faith, if it had not believed before o earned good in its faith, when the sun rises from the West, Dajjal, and the beast of the earth (Tabari).

This is an issue, what is that time and sign when *Iman* or repentance will not be acceptable if a person did not do this before?

In *Hadith* #2, it is mentioned as sunrise. In *Hadith* #3 it is mentioned that sunrise, and the beast will appear one after the other, while in *Hadith* #4, sunrise, *Dajjal*, and the beast are mentioned, when these three will appear, then belief has no benefit for one who did not believe before. This is also mentioned in the *Hadith* that *Isa* [Jesus] will kill *Dajjal*, and in the time of *Isa* (Jesus) there will be people with *Iman* (true belief) only.

So, either the appearance of *Dajjal* and *Isa* will be before sunrise from the west, or after that, the sun will rise from the west, the gate for the acceptance of *Iman* and repentance will be closed. In a *Hadith* it is mentioned that this sunrise will be the first sign. So, the scholars explained that the gates would be closed for some time after the sunrise from the West, and later with the return of *Isa* (Jesus) they will get open again. Some scholars said that, after all these major signs, the gate would be closed.

So, the meaning of

> *"the first ever sign"*

is the first ever for closure of the gate.

Hafiz Ibn Hajar said,

> *"After sunrise from the west, the world will remain for 120 years."*

This type of sunrise is indication that the natural system has taken reverse, so the *Shariah*-based rules also change, and *Iman* and repentance is not acceptable now. Regarding the beast, *Allah* said in the verse of *Holy Quran*,

> *"And when the word [decree] is fulfilled against them, we shall bring out from the earth, a beast for them to speak to them because mankind believed not with certainly in our Ayat [signs/rules] (27:82)."*

Further details concerning that beast are given in following *Ahadith*.

HADITH #5:

Ibn Juraij reported that *Ibn Az Zubair* described the beast and said;

> *Its head is like that of a bull, its eyes are like those of a pig. Its ears are like those of an elephant, its horns are like the horns of stags, its neck is like that of an ostrich, its chest is like that of a lion, its color is like a tiger, its hunches are like those of a cat, its tail is like the tail of a ram, and its legs are like a camel's. Between each pair of its joints is a distance of twelve cubits. It will bring out with it the staff of Musa (Moses) and the ring of Sulayman [Solomon]. He will stamp a white spot on the face of every believer using the staff of Musa. This white spot will spread on the face, and the face will shine white. Similarly, he will stamp a black spot on the face of every disbeliever using the ring of Sulayman. This black spot will spread on the face, and the face will become black. When the people trade with one another in the market places, they will say, "How much is this, O believer?" Or "How much is this, O disbeliever?" Then the beast will say, "O so-and-so, enjoy yourself, for you are among the people of paradise and it will say, "O so-and-so, you are among the people of hell."*

This means that *Dajjal, Isa* and all other signs will appear before the emergence of the beast and the sunrise from the West. At this time the gate will be closed for *Iman* and *Taubah*.

Regarding the smoke mentioned in *Hadith* #1, some scholars said that this smoke is mentioned in verse ten of Chapter 44 of the *Holy Quran*.

> *"Wait for the day when the sky will bring forth a visible smoke [44:10]."*

Some people said, the smoke mentioned in this *Ayat* was what occurred to the people of *Makkah* in the time of famine. In any case, the smoke as a sign of *Qiyamat* is mentioned in *Ahadith*.

HADITH #6:

Ibn Jareer narrated from *Huzaifah Ibn Yaman* that the *Prophet Muhammad* said,

> *"The first ever signs are appearing of Dajjal, the return of Isa, and a fire. This will emerge from the midst of And [a city in Yemen]. This will drive the people to "Mahshar" [place of their assembling for accountability] taking rest with where they will take it and the smoke."*

Huzaifah Ibn Yaman asked *Prophet Muhammad* about smoke. *Prophet Muhammad* recited the above verse (44:10) and said, it will cover and fill up from east to west for 40 days and nights (*Ibn Jareer*).

THE RETURN OF JESUS [*ISA*]

Considering the history of the *Israelite Jewish* tribes it is clear that *Allah* blessed them with the message of hundreds of *Prophets*. Before *Prophet Musa* (Moses) they were deprived of their fundamental rights in Egypt, they were enslaved by Pharaoh and tortured severely. *Prophet Musa* (Moses) came to liberate them from the clutches of slavery. *Allah* drowned *Firaun* and his people, but they refused to go to *Syria*, their own land, due to their cowardice. They were sent to *Sinai*; later they came to *Syria* where *Talut*, *Dawud*, and *Sulaiman* ruled *Syria*. After *Sulaiman*, once again they lost everything and they were attacked by others, killed imprisoned, enslaved and deprived of everything. The *Prophet* gave them happy news that there will be a *Messiah* (one who will renew and reform their religion, which they have disfigured according to their wishes) who comes to them. They will once again get rid of this disgrace and humiliation.

They were waiting for a *Messiah* who would come with a big army, who would conquer this whole area and establish a great Israeli state, but when *Prophet Isa* (Jesus) came without what they had been expecting, they denied him. He was born without a father, and they blamed him as the son of *Yusuf Al Najjar* (Joseph of Nazareth) and planned to assassinate him. *Allah* raised him up to the heavens alive. The Jews until now are waiting for the promised *Messiah*.

Allah said in *Holy Quran*:

> "Because of breaking their covenant, and of their rejecting the Ayat of Allah, and of their killing the Prophets unjustly, and of their saying our hearts are wrapped [so we cannot hear and understand of filled up with belief and knowledge, so we do not need you and your teaching] Nay, Allah has set a seal upon their hearts because of their disbelief, so they believe not but a little [or a few of them]. And because of their disbelief and saying [putting] against Maryam a false charge [of fornication and illegitimate son], and their saying [claiming] that we have killed the Messiah, Isa son of Maryam, the Messenger of (Allah said) while they have not killed him, nor crucified him. But it only seemed to them [they have done it or it means that the resemblance of Isa was put over another man and they killed him]. And those who hold conflicting views there on are indeed confused. They have no [certain] knowledge, they follow nothing but conjecture. For surely, they killed him not, but Allah raised him up onto himself and Allah is all powerful, all wise (4:153-158)."

So, *Isa* (Jesus) was raised up to heaven and he will come back. This return is mentioned in dozens of authentic *Ahadith* and this accepted and approved by the entire *ummah* for the last fifteen hundred years. If someone rejects this concept he will lose his *Iman*.

HADITH #1:

Prophet Muhammad said, as narrated by *Abu Huraira*,

> "By one in whose hand there is my soul, surely the son of Maryam will come down amongst you as a just ruler, so he will break the cross, and kill the pig, [meaning he will drop the disfigured concept of Christianity and will confirm its abrogation, wrong concept of crucifixion and eating pork] and he will drop [finish] the battle [as disbelief will disappear totally] and he will pour [in abundance]. The wealth that no one will accept (Zakat) and one sajdah (prostration) will be better [for one] than the world and all the things therein [Muslim, Tirmidhi, Bukhari, Ahmad]."

HADITH #2:

Abu Hurairah narrated *Prophet Muhammad* said,

> "How will you be? When the son of Maryam will come down to you and your Imam will be from amongst you [Muslim, Bukhari, Ahmad]."

HADITH #3:

Jabir son of *Abdullah* narrated,

"The Prophet said, Isa [Jesus] son of Maryam [Mary] will come down amongst you, the Ameer [leader] will ask Isa [Jesus] to lead the prayer. He will say, no, you are the leader for one another. The honor Allah has given you people [Ahmad, Muslim]."

JESUS'S (*ISA'S*) MIRACLES

It is not a must for a *Messenger* to show miracles, nor the miracle is in the hands of a *Prophet*, and neither can he show that on his own will.

Allah said,

> *"This is not for a Messenger to bring forth a sign [miracle] but by the leave of Allah. Every appointed term is written [there with Allah. He gives the same to someone in its appointed time and space] (13:38)."*

Miracles are metaphysical and that is why some people deny them while others think the person concerned is either God or a partner of God, or a part of god or even his reflection. All these are wrong concepts. *Allah* has the perfect and irresistible power to do anything he wills. Then *Allah* gives to a *Messenger* a miracle or miracles according to the circumstances and situation concerned, such a thing which is far better than the expertise they have at that time, to defeat them, having no power to counter that miracle.

So, he gave *Ibrahim* (Abraham) and *Musa* (Moses) such miracles, which defeated the sorcerers, the magicians, and the practitioners of witchcraft. *Isa* [Jesus] was given miracles that defeated the utmost skillful physicians of that time, while the medical field of that time had discovered the medicine and treatment for almost every disease, but not for one born blind and for leprosy. Nor they could breathe into a non-living entity and make it alive or to give life to dead or to inform his colleagues about their food they will be eating or storing. But *Isa* [Jesus] was doing this sometime whenever *Allah* willed as *Allah* said:

> *"And [Allah send him i.e. Jesus] as a Messenger to the children of Israel [saying] indeed I have come to you people with a sign from your Lord, that I will design for you from clay figure [shape and structure] of a bird and breath into it and it will become a bird by the leave of Allah, and I heal the born and blind and the leper [one who is suffering of Leucoedema], and I bring dead to life by the leave of Allah, and I inform you of what you eat and what you store in you houses, surely therein is a sign for you, if you believe (3:49)."*

With all his miracles he [Jesus] said

> *"with by the leave of Allah"*

means that Jesus is subjected to *Allah* that none of these things I have done on my own nor I can do it.

DAY OF JUDGEMENT AND JESUS [*ISA*]

The *Day of Judgment* is the day which everyone would be put to question and to accountability, the *Messengers* and those to whom they were sent as *Allah* said,

> *"The day when we shall call together all human beings with their Imam [their Prophet or with their records of deeds or with the book which was sent down to them or with the leaders they followed them] [17:71]."*

He said:

> *"How [will it be] then when we will bring from each nation a witness and we will bring you [O Muhammad] as a witness against these people [4:41]."*

Also, *Allah* said:

> *"On the day when Allah will gather the Messengers together [on the day of judgment] and say to them, what was the response you received from people? They will say, we have no knowledge; verily you are the all knower*

of the hidden [unknown things]. [Remember] when Allah will say [on the day of judgment] O Isa [Jesus] son of Maryam [Mary] remember my favor to you and to your mother as I have supported you with "Ruh Ul Quds" [the Holy Spirit] you spoke to people, in the cradle and you in "Kahulat" and as I taught you the Kitab [or Kitabat means writing] and wisdom, the Taurat[Torah] and Injeel [Gospel] and as you were creating [making] from clay the image of a bird and it was becoming a bird with my leave and you were healing the born blind and the leper[one who was suffering from Leucoedema] with my leave, and as you were giving life to dead with my leave and as I restrained the children of Israel from you [to kill you] when you came to them with clear signs [rules and laws bringing Torah back to its origin and they disliked it] so those who disbelieved they said, this is an evident magic [lie]. And when I revealed to the "Hawariyyun" [disciples] to believe in me and in my Messenger, so they said, we believed. So, bear witness that we are Muslims and [remember] when the "Hawariyyun" [disciples] said, O Isa [Jesus] son of Maryam [Mary], can your Lord send down to us a Ma'ida [tray /table of food] from the heaven? He said, fear Allah if you are believer. They said, we want to eat therefrom and to make our hearts satisfied and to know that you have told us the truth and that we may be witness to it. Isa [Jesus] son of Maryam [Mary] said, O Allah! Our Lord! Send us from the heaven a "Ma'ida" [tray or table full of food] to be "Eid" [festival] for the first and last of us [means those who are there now and those who will be coming after us] and [to be] a sign from your side. And provide us with provision and you are the best of the providers. Allah said, I am going to send it down unto them, but if any of you later on disbelieved, then I will punish him with such a torment, I will not inflict on anyone among the people and [remember] when Allah will say to Isa [on the day of judgment], O Isa [Jesus] son of Maryam [Mary] did you say to people, take [believe] me and my mother two gods besides Allah [means with him, so there may be three gods]? He will say, Glory be to you it was not for me to say what I had no right [to say]. If I would have said such a thing, then you would have known it for sure. You know what is in myself and I do not know what is in yourself. Verily you are the All-Knower of hidden [unknown] things. I have never said to them but what you have commanded me with, to worship Allah, my Lord and your Lord, and I was a witness over them, as long as I was living there amongst them. Then when you withdrew me [to yourself], you were the watcher over them and you are a witness to everything. If you punish them, so they are your slaves and if you will forgive them then you are the All-Mighty, All-Wise. Allah will say, this is a day on which the truthful will profit for their truth. For them there are gardens beneath which rivers flow. They shall abide therein forever. Allah is pleased with them and they pleased with them. That is the great success to Allah belongs the dominion of the heavens and the earth, and all that is therein and he has the power to do anything (5:110-120)."

This whole process will take place to make it clear to those who believed in *Isa* [Jesus] in another way, means as god, son of god, part of god, or a partner with him and those who believed in his mother the like of this, as certain groups believed in the trinity, three gods, three entities constitute god, or each one of these three entities is God. These three are God, Jesus and *Ruh Ul Qudus* [the *Holy Ghost* or *Holy Spirit*] and to some the Virgin Mary instead of the holy ghost. Also, the statement is in the context of questioning Jesus and his answer to make it clear that Jesus has never said of his lordship or worship.

This is what *Allah* said:

> *"And when Isa [Jesus] came with clear proofs [miracles, statements, rules] he said, Indeed I have come to you people with wisdom [Prophethood] and to make clear to you some of which you differ therein. So, fear Allah and obey me. Verily Allah is my Lord and your Lord, so worship him. This is the straight path, then the groups [sects] differed amongst them, so woe to those who do wrong from the torment of the painful day. Do they then wait for the hour, which will come to them suddenly, while they will perceive not. Friends on that day will be foes to one another, but not the pious people. [He will say to the believers] o my slaves! No fear is on you nor shall you grieve, those who believed in our verse and they are submissive (43:63-69)."*

There are 10's of *Ahadith* in this regard, which proves the return of *Isa*, keeping in view all these *Ahadith* and *Ayat* several points have become clear.

1.

Isa (Jesus) is born of his mother *Maryam* without a father. Botanically or zoologically this process is called self-pollination or parthenogenesis, where both male and female sperms exist in one body. Even though *Isa* was born as a miracle, but still there is a physical possibility of such like birth as well.

2.

Isa (Jesus) has not been killed or crucified.

3.

He has been raised up to the heaven physically.

4.

He was raised up to the heaven, when he was a young man of 33 years. He will return as is, as changes are not taking place when one is out of space and time. Upon his return he will perform as a jurist of *Muhammad's Shariah* and have children.

5.

Upon his return, he will be the follower of the *Prophet Muhammad*. He will pray his first prayer behind the *Imam* of this *Ummah*. Later on as an *Alim* and *Mujtahid* of *Islamic Shariah*, he will lead the prayers as well.

6.

He will drop *Jizya* [a tax upon Non-*Muslims* in a *Muslim* state] and *Kharaj* [a tax on Non-*Muslims* agricultural land]. This means the *Islamic*

State will protect their lives, properties, and faith, and they will support the state as the *Muslim* citizens give certain financial rituals like *Zakat* and *Fitra*. When Isa will come back he will drop these because the state will be rich enough. In a hadith it is said, that the wealth will be in abundance, it would mean no protection based on *Jizya* and *Kharaj*. This means the *Prophet Muhammad* has limited the law of *Jizya* and *Kharaj* up to the return of *Isa*.

7.

Isa (Jesus) will kill *Dajjal* [Antichrist / imposter], *Muslim* will only occupy the world as a whole and justice and peace will prevail.

8.

Isa (Jesus) will kill the pigs and he will break the cross. The Christians believe in his crucifixion as expiation, they also believe that *Isa* used to graze pigs and eat them. This action will reject the two concepts of Christians, and Christianity will not remain except *Islam*. This is proven from a *Mutawatir Hadith* and *Mutawatir* means, successive *Hadith* and the successive generations adapted the same as their faith. Rejection of this type of *Hadith* is disbelief.

9.

Isa (Jesus) will remain in the world for 45 years [he was 33 years when he was raised to heaven, this means he will stay twelve more years, which will make 45 years, or this means that he will live an additional 45 years]. After he passes away he will be buried with the *Prophet Muhammad*. On the *Day of Judgment*, he will come out with the *Prophet Muhammad*, *Abu Bakr*, and *Omar* will be on either side of them. Narrated by *Ibn Jawzi* from *Abdullah Ibn Amir*.

10.

In the time of *Isa* [Jesus] there will be no hatred, no enmity, jealousy, as everything will be available to everyone and the world will be like that of paradise.

May *Allah* guide us to the right path and right beliefs and empower us to practice righteous good deeds, which will please *Allah* and will make our life in this world a satisfied one and in the hereafter a pleasant one. *Amin.*

BOOKS BY *QAZI FAZL ULLAH*

Qazi Fazl Ullah has written other books. Below is a short list with summaries.

FIQH KEE TAREEKH WA IRTIQA (URDU)

Islam is *Deen* (religion) and is a complete code of life. Its laws are of two types, textual and deduced, but how the text is interpreted and how laws are deduced therefrom is called *"Jurisprudence"* and the laws are called *Fiqh,* and how this *Fiqh* got developed and compiled. This book gives the details about its stages of development.

MOHAMMADUR RASOOLULLAH (URDU)

The biography of the *Prophet Muhammad* was preserved from day one by his blessed companions. Then scholars and historians have written books in this regard in different times, both concise and detailed. This book on the biography of *Prophet Muhammad* is an excellent balance of concise and detailed, as a concise a book sometimes misses things and people do not have time to read and understand too detailed a book. Another important feature of this book is that almost with every important part of the *Prophet's* biography, the relevant part of the *Holy Quran* has been quoted, which illustrates that the *Prophet's* life was the practical shape of the *Holy Book*.

SARMAYA DARANA NIZAM ISHTIRAKIYAT AUR ISLAM (URDU)

Humans, throughout their history, have thought ahead and planned their economics and economical needs. They created systems for these purposes. The three systems most widely practiced in history are capitalism, communism, and *Islam*. This book is a comparative study of these 3 economical systems and it proves that the *Islamic* system bestowed upon us by the Creator is the best one with regard to justice and no room for exploitation.

DAWAT O JIHAD (URDU)

The basic duty of every *Prophet* and his followers was and is to call the people towards *Allah* in a peaceful, attractive, and convincing way, and wherever and whenever they encountered resistance and hindrances in this regard, they must remove these hindrances. At times, this leads to fights, as when the conspiracy is big and the opponents try to take away their fundamental rights, so they have the right to defend it but how, when, and where? In this book, it is mentioned that *Islam* teaches us to convey, convince, and convert, but not to coerce. This book is an answer to anti-*Islamic* propaganda, especially about the concept of *Jihad* in *Islam*.

ISLAM AUR SIYASAT (URDU)

Islam and Politics—as it is known from the title that this book discusses *Islamic* political system, because *Islam* is *Deen*, meaning a complete code of life and not a set of a few rituals. It has its own system for state and government. So, wherever *Muslims* are in power, if they will implement this system, they meet the needs of everyone, regardless of color, caste, or religion. *Islam* covers the details, such as how to elect a government, and how to run the state to provide peace and justice to all.

RIYASATI ISLAMI KA TASWWAR (URDU)

The title means the concept of an *Islamic* state, and *"concept"* means its conduct. In this book, it is mentioned how and why a state and government is needed, and how that state and government may be and should be run. The Creator *Allah* the Almighty knows all our needs, necessities, qualities and shortcomings, so the system he has given is the only system that can ensure people's security and safety and can provide them peace and justice, making the state a welfare state.

USOOLUT - TAFSEER (ARABIC)

Every branch of science has its own rules, principles and methodologies, which provide guidelines for explaining it and how to interpret it, so this methodology is a circle or limits one may keep himself confines to so he will not get lost or go astray.

This book covers the explanation of the *Holy Quran*, the last and final book of *Allah*. The book of *Allah* is the basic source of *Islam* and *Islamic* law, so its explanation requires certain rules to be followed in its explanation, so one may not be unbridled and without restraint, otherwise he will put his faith in danger.

DIRAYATUR RIWAYAH (ARABIC)

Hadith (sayings, actions and sanctions) of *Prophet Muhammad* is the second fundamental source of *Islam* and *Islamic* laws and also it is the interpretation of the *Holy Quran*. The companions of the *Prophet Muhammad* have preserved them in their memories and in their scriptures and the second and third generation took it from them and preserved them as well. Later on, when there was a fear of perversion, then these *Ahadith* were compiled officially and later on, the authentic scholars gathered them together in various books. Furthermore, critics compiled a biography of all these narrators and put certain rules about how a *Hadith* could be accepted. This book includes all these details.

HUJJIYATI HADITH (URDU)

This book is regarding the authenticity of *Hadith* of the *Prophet*, as there is a baseless propaganda that *Hadith* were not written in the time of the *Prophet*, but later on, making them unreliable. This is wrong, as

Sahaba used to write *Ahadith* and sometimes the *Prophet* himself used to order them to write. But they trusted their memory more than writing. Official compilation took place later on, when *Muslim* rulers became aware of the weakness of people's memories and the loss of those individuals writing. This book provides all these details and makes it clear that *Hadith* is *Wahi* (Revelation) and source of *Islamic Shariah* (Law).

FUNDAMENTALISM, SECULARISM AUR ISLAM (URDU)

Propaganda is being spread either because of ignorance or with mala fide intention that *Islam* is fundamentalism.

Fundamentalism was a term used for Christianity when it blocked the ways of scientific research, invention and development, and some people wanted to adopt it as a basic guideline for states and government. So those who were with research and development branded that as fundamentalism. But *Islam* does not stop or block progress and research; rather, it encourages it and even orders scholars to go ahead and do research, as discussed in this book.

AL IJTIHADU WAT TAQLEED (URDU)

Humans are social and intellectual animals. They have all the same needs as animals, but they are distinct from them because of their intellect as they are looking for their ease, to do a little and get a lot. For this purpose, some intellectuals invent things and others follow them. Then as they are bound to obey the *Deen* of *Allah*, there are other intellectuals who deduce laws from its fundamental sources: the *Quran* and the *Sunnah*, and the less intellectuals follow them, as they should. This is the only intellectual and reasonable way. This book explains this issue and its importance.

MUSALMAN AURAT (URDU)

Allah created the world. He created humans and made them men and women. He gave different qualities to both genders for the smooth running of this life to depend upon each other, but as humans they are equal. Some women made history and they did memorable work that many men could not have done. This small book mentions some of the great work of some great women, particularly *Muslim* women, to make it clear that *Islam* deeply respects women and appreciates their contributions to society.

ASMATI RASOOL OR ZAWAJI AAISHA (URDU)

This world is a combination of opposites and some people have been given a great status. The *Messengers* of *Allah* are the chosen and beloved of *Allah*. He made them and built them up for himself and his work. They are the most respected and honored people, and they must be given respect, as any disgrace to them can harm the feelings and sentiments of their followers, which can cause trouble. In this book this issue is discussed, as well as a misconception about the *Prophet's* marriage to *Aaisha*; namely, that she was minor at that time. Academically and research fully, this book corrects this misconception.

AL FARA'ID FIL AQA'ID (ARABIC)

Aqeedah and *Aqa'id* means faith and beliefs, respectively, and they are the base of *Deen*. Certain beliefs are the contents of *Iman*. What is important for a *Muslim* to believe? These are detailed in this concise book. Some *Muslim* sects have misconstrued some of these beliefs, so the book mentions that as well and makes the right faith clear.

QAWA'IDUT - TAJWEED (ARABIC)

One of the basic duties of the *Prophet* was to teach his followers how to recite the holy book properly. His *Sahabah* learnt it from him and then this became a specific science in future generations. They not only taught their students the proper way of recitation, they also wrote books about it. This science is called *Tajweed*, which literally means to make good, but in this science, it means to recite good. This book prescribes the basic rules for *Tajweed* as proper pronunciation not only makes the words and sounds good but also helps in giving the proper meaning of the word.

AL QAWA'IDUL FIQHIYAH (ARABIC)

Islam is *Deen* and a complete system and code of life. For each and every aspect of life there are rules and laws in *Islam*. Some of these rules are in text of the *Quran* and the *Sunnah*, while some others are deduced therefrom. For deduction, the authentic jurists have laid down rules of deduction and the qualities required for themselves. Then, after deduction, they have found some commonalities in different laws in different chapters, so they laid down a common rule for that and these rules called *Al Qawa'idul - Fiqhiyah*, or legal maxims, which make the study of *Fiqh* easy and understandable. This book includes some known and famous legal maxims in all four schools of jurisprudence.

AL JIHAD FIL ISLAM (ARABIC)

Jihad is a very important issue in *Islam*; to defend life, property, honor and faith is not only a well-known right in each and every culture but also a duty in *Islam*, but how and when? This book is written on this subject. As this issue is quite controversial, this is a reasonable answer to these questions in the light of the *Quran* and *Sunnah*.

MAULANA UBAIDULLAH SINDHI (URDU)

Maulana Ubaidullah Sindhi, originally from a *Sikh* family, accepted *Islam* when he was a teenager. He studied *Deen* in the proper and traditional way, then joined the freedom movement. He went through a lot of difficulties, and lived in exile for 24 years. As a revolutionary leader, he is controversial and many people wrote against him as well as for him. This book describes his personality, struggle, and thoughts to know who he was and how he was.

ASMATI RASOOL AND KHATMI NUBUWWAT (URDU)

Asmati Rasool and *Khatmi Nubuwwat* are reasonable and logical. This book consists of two parts. The defense of the *Prophet* and that of him being the last and final *Prophet* of *Allah* is a reasonable and logical thing, as *Allah* sent *Messengers* in different times to different areas and different nations, and when they worked in their respected times in those areas, *Allah* sent the *Prophet Muhammad* to the entire world to combine their work and bring humanity together on the same theme, subject and faith that all those earlier *Messengers* were sent for. This book is a concise, detailed and logical interpretation of this finality.

SAYYIDAH AAISHA'S AGE AT MARRIAGE (ENGLISH)

Islam is a Natural *Deen* or *Deen* of Nature. This is a balanced *Deen* providing a comprehensive justice system, and the *Holy Prophet* is the perfect role model as a perfect human. His words, actions, and sanctions are the proper interpretation of the *Holy Quran* and the second fundamental source of laws in *Islam*. There is a commonly held belief, especially among critics of *Islam*, that the *Prophet* married *Aaisha* when she was only nine years of age. In this book, all the details about this issue is given that how this word *Tis'aa* (which means nine) happened there and what the real story is to counter the false accounts and correct the record.

JIHAD IN ISLAM : WHY, HOW, AND WHEN?

(ENGLISH)

Jihad as a word in *Arabic* means struggle or striving hard, especially for a noble cause, while as a term in *Islam*, it specifically means to fight in the path/cause of *Allah*. But when does this fight happen? When it is inevitable and unavoidable as the very integrity of a state, the lives of its citizens or the very ideology is facing a big danger. But a very baseless smear campaign is going on against *Jihad* and it is branded as a synonym to terrorism, so this book is a must to make the true concept of *Jihad* clear and counter the propaganda.

SHARIA AND POLITICS (ENGLISH)

Islam is *Deen* and *Deen* means a complete system and a perfect code of life as this is given by the very creator of the worlds, who knows all about his creatures, their qualities and their shortcomings, and can provide a perfect solution to their problems. But unfortunately, some people have been doing wrong in the name of *Khalafat* and presenting their wrong idea as the *Islamic* political system, so there was great need of a book that can present the proper shape of an *Islamic* state and *Islamic* political system given by the Creator; when executed properly, it is actually a mercy and blessing for the creatures. This book explains this concept clearly.

HAJJ & UMRAH IN ALL FOUR SCHOOLS OF JURISPRUDENCE (ENGLISH)

Hajj (pilgrimage to *Mecca*) is one of the Five Pillars of *Islam* and a very important but a complicated type of *Ibadah* (worship) as *Muslims* from all around the world get together to perform it together. They follow the interpretation of their *Imams* (jurists), so sometimes they look at others when they do not perform a specific virtue the way they do, then they think they are doing wrong, which is not so, but all of them are performing correctly according to the interpretation of their *Imams*. This book gives all these details in sequence according to all four *Imams* the *Muslim Ummah* follows.

MOON SIGHTING, SALATUL TARAWEEH AND SALATUL WITR (ENGLISH)

The *Islamic* Calendar is lunar-based. Its different *Ibadaat* time is based on moon-sighting; the lunar month starts with the new moon. Even though astronomy tells us what day the moon will be born (i.e., new) with perfect accuracy, discerning on which day it will be visible in a specific area is still not accurate. That is why differences in opinion happen all over the world, and should we to go by the calendar or by a sighting?

Also, at *Ramadan*, which is the most important month in *Islam* as a mandatory *Ibadah*, fasting is mandatory as well, but there is an extra, highly recommended *Ibadah,* the *Taraweeh,* but how many *Rakat* should we pray? *Muslims* differ about this. Another important *Ibadah* is *Salat Ul Witr*. We use this prayer all year, but during *Ramadan* this is prayed in *Jama'at* and different *Imams* have different opinions regarding the number of *Rakats* and its procedure. So, this book gives all the details about these three important issues.

SCIENCE OF HADITH (ENGLISH)

Hadith is the second fundamental source of *Islamic* law. They are the words, actions and sanctions of the *Holy Prophet*. To record all these in memory and writing, to compile it and to record the biography of those narrators who did this great job and this is considered as a miracle of the *Prophet*. But the enemies of *Islam* used to create doubts in this regard. This book is written on this subject, and it is enough an answer to all the objections that people made from different angles.

ABOUT THE AUTHOR

Qazi Fazl Ullah is an American philosopher, linguist, and author. He is *Fazil Wafaqul Madaris* where he studied *Arabic* grammar, *Arabic* literature, *Fiqh*, jurisprudence, logic, philosophy, *Ilmul Kalam, Seerah, Tafseer, Hadith,* and *Islamic* history. He studied at *Peshawar University* and *Islamic University Islamabad* in *Pakistan* and specialized in law, economics, and political science. He has taught all these subjects in *Pakistan* and the United States at different institutions. He was elected as a *National Assembly Parliamentarian* in *Pakistan*. He worked in underserved areas to provide jobs, build infrastructure, schools, museums, public health facilities, and increase communication technologies as the chair of the *Social Action Board*. He has traveled extensively throughout the Middle East, North Africa, Europe, South East Asia, North and Central America. He has given seminars in various parts of the world in these subjects. He speaks and has given lectures and seminars in *Urdu, Pashto, Farsi,* English, and *Arabic*. He has published works in *Pashto, Urdu, Arabic,* and English internationally. He has given the complete *Tafsir Ul Quran* in *Pashto* multiple times in *Pakistan*. He has also given *Tafsir Ul Quran* in *Urdu, Pashto,* and English in the United States. It includes *Usul Ul Fiqh, Usul Ul Mirath, Hadith al Qudsi, Hadith an Nabawi* in English on multiple occasions. He considers himself a student to continue acquisitions of knowledge. He is currently leading *Tafsir Ul Quran, Usual Al Fiqh, Seerat Un Nabi,* Science of Inheritance (*Mirath*) in English and *Al*

Mukhtar Lil Fatawa, Dirayat Ul Riwaya in *Arabic* in Los Angeles, California.

www.ingramcontent.com/pod-product-compliance
Lightning Source LLC
Chambersburg PA
CBHW020807160426
43192CB00006B/477